# I Had a Great Time!

## Mary Elizabeth Salzmann

Consulting Editor Monica Marx, M.A./Reading Specialist

Published by SandCastle™, an imprint of ABDO Publishing Company, 4940 Viking Drive, Edina, Minnesota 55435.

Printed in the United States.

Credits
Edited by: Pam Price
Curriculum Coordinator: Nancy Tuminelly
Cover and Interior Design and Production: Mighty Media
Photo Credits: Brand X Pictures, Comstock, Corbis Images, Digital Vision, Image 100, ImageState, PhotoDisc, Stockbyte

Library of Congress Cataloging-in-Publication Data

Salzmann, Mary Elizabeth, 1968-
    I had a great time! / Mary Elizabeth Salzmann.
        p. cm. -- (Sight words)
    Includes index.
    Summary: Uses simple sentences, photographs, and a brief story to introduce six different words: about, get, I, one, us, work.
    ISBN 1-59197-477-1
    1. Readers (Primary) 2. Vocabulary--Juvenile literature. [1. Reading.] I. Title. II. Series.

PE1119.S234228 2003
728.1--dc21
                                                        2003050321

SandCastle™ books are created by a professional team of educators, reading specialists, and content developers around five essential components that include phonemic awareness, phonics, vocabulary, text comprehension, and fluency. All books are written, reviewed, and leveled for guided reading, early intervention reading, and Accelerated Reader® programs and designed for use in shared, guided, and independent reading and writing activities to support a balanced approach to literacy instruction.

## Let Us Know

After reading the book, SandCastle would like you to tell us your stories about reading. What is your favorite page? Was there something hard that you needed help with? Share the ups and downs of learning to read. We want to hear from you! To get posted on the ABDO Publishing Company Web site, send us e-mail at:

**sandcastle@abdopub.com**

**SandCastle Level: Beginning**

# Featured Sight Words

about    get

I    one

us    work

Kay and Troy read about Spain.

Cate and Mary are going to get some ice cream.

I have a friend
named Len.

Ruth and Faye share one end of the seesaw.

There are six of us
in a circle.

Paul and Trish work together in the library.

# My Friend's Party

I am at a party with my friends.

Just about everyone wears a costume.

We get to play fun games.

We work hard to win prizes.

Then each one of us has a big piece of cake.

I am having a great time!

# More Sight Words in This Book

| | |
|---|---|
| a | of |
| and | some |
| are | the |
| at | then |
| has | there |
| have | to |
| in | we |
| just | with |
| my | |

All words identified as sight words in this book are from Edward Bernard Fry's "First Hundred Instant Sight Words."

# Picture Index

**cake,** p. 20

**circle,** p. 13

**ice cream,** p. 7

**library,** p. 15

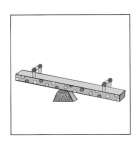

**seesaw,** p. 11

**Spain,** p. 5

# About SandCastle™

A professional team of educators, reading specialists, and content developers created the SandCastle™ series to support young readers as they develop reading skills and strategies and increase their general knowledge. The SandCastle™ series has four levels that correspond to early literacy development in young children. The levels are provided to help teachers and parents select the appropriate books for young readers.

**Emerging Readers**
(no flags)

**Beginning Readers**
(1 flag)

**Transitional Readers**
(2 flags)

**Fluent Readers**
(3 flags)

These levels are meant only as a guide. All levels are subject to change.

To see a complete list of SandCastle™ books and other nonfiction titles from ABDO Publishing Company, visit www.abdopub.com or contact us at:
4940 Viking Drive, Edina, Minnesota 55435 • 1-800-800-1312 • fax: 1-952-831-1632